PRAISE FOR RE
WONKY th

'It was fantastic!
Max, age 9, The Cockpit Theatre

'Absolutely amazing!!'
10yo, Courtyard Arts Centre

'Joe and Willow's boundless energy and engaging style will keep children of all ages hooked'
Headteacher, Lowther Primary

***SUDDENLY...!* AND OTHER STORIES chapter book**

'Moving, witty and inventive, these stories capture your imagination as well as your heart. Inspiring for kids of all ages... I loved every minute'
Alison Steadman, actress and children's author

'Bursting with energy... a perfect read aloud book for parents and teachers, as well as a jolly exciting set of adventures for independent readers'
Chicken & Frog Children's Bookshop

***SUDDENLY...!* audiobook**

Customer review, Waterstones

'A rip-roaring audiobook... non-stop adventure featuring delicious wordplay'
Kentish Towner

Poetry versus Pottery
by
Rapper Scool Yo
featuring
Pete
(my best mate)

by Joe Bromley

illustrated by Rosie Alabaster

featuring characters from *WONKY*

the show by Joe Bromley and Willow Nash

Really Big Pants Theatre Company

POETRY VERSUS POTTERY first published in 2019

© Joe Bromley 2019

Illustrations © Rosie Alabaster 2019
rosiealabaster.com

ISBN 978-1-9999461-1-1

A really big thank to the lovely team at the Castelnau Centre Project in Barnes, London for supporting us with *WONKY* and hosting its launch in 2018

Congratulations to Hannah from Brentwood on winning the Name the Ninth Peg competition! See your peg on page 45

And we couldn't resist naming the news reporter on page 78 Rosalind, for Diane Roome's first granddaughter ('a joy and already a determined soul')

The page used for the blackout poetry on page 47 is from our chapter book, *SUDDENLY...! AND OTHER STORIES*

Sunflower picture on page 77 is by Joe's sister, Jane. She's ace

A CIP catalogue record for this book is available from the British Library

All rights reserved. No part of this publication may be reproduced, stored in or introduced into a retrieval system, or transmitted, in any form or by any means (electronic, mechanical, photocopying, recording or otherwise), without the prior written permission of the publisher. This book is sold subject to the condition that it shall not be resold, lent, hired out or otherwise circulated without the prior consent of the publisher

The moral rights of the author have been asserted

This is a work of fiction. Names, characters, businesses, places, events, and incidents are either the products of the author's imagination or used in a fictitious manner. Any resemblance to actual persons, living or dead, or actual events is entirely coincidental

Printed and bound in Great Britain

Orphans Press Ltd
Arrow Close, Leominster Enterprise Park
Leominster, Herefordshire HR6 0LD
Tel 01568 612460 orphans.co.uk

For Elliot aka Boy Wonder

*Here's to poets and potters everywhere
(and painters and pie-eaters
and partygoers and potato-growers.
Oh, and really-big-pants-wearers)*

Really Big Pants is a theatre company specifically for primary-aged children. We wrote our show, *WONKY*, as a response to the growing (no pun intended) crisis that an increasing number of children did not know where their food came from or that vegetables were grown in the ground. That was our starting point, together with the value of so-called 'ugly' veg that was deemed unsuitable for sale and consumption. We then linked this to peer pressure issues and gender equality, along with the challenges of being 'different', and the seed for *WONKY* was sown.

It soon became clear that we were having so much fun channelling the character of Rapper Scool Yo and rapping in rehearsals, that we wanted to use his voice to unleash some poetry. Which then became a platform for ALL the characters to unleash their voices. So here's a collection of poems, cheek by jowl with some visual glory from Rosie Alabaster (channelling Rapper Scool Yo's best mate, Pete).

Happy reading.

Joe and Willow
Really Big Pants

PS We've been shown round some incredible edible playgrounds in schools and it's wonderful to see children connecting with nature and learning how to grow food and develop a healthy attitude to nutrition

PPS There are activity sheets and resource packs on our website – have a look at reallybigpants.co.uk

PPPS A really big thank you to all the awesome audiences who have come to see our shows. If you haven't seen us live in action yet – either in a venue near you or at your school – be quick! Before our knees pack up

Contents

Poetry hintroduction by Rapper Scool Yo	p12
Pottery introduction by Pete (including a teapot)	p14
'My grandma says my grammar is happalling'	p17
A poem from Trixie	p18
A Toby Jug	p19
'Pete is making some pots for me to grow herbs in'	p20
A bee hotel	p21
A poem from Miss Squelch	p22
Plant label sticks	p24
'When I was at school, I did not like science'	p26
A thimble	p28
A limerick from Coach Outback	p29
A sonnet from the headteacher	p30
A frame	p31
A poem from the dinner lady	p33
A fridge magnet	p34
'Clamber'	p35
A poem from Messy Jesse's mam	p36
A poem from Messy Jesse	p38
Wind chimes	p39
'Yo. I is a rapper, and I is a boy'	p40

A poem from Messy Jesse's dance teacher	p42
Coat pegs	p44
Blackout poetry	p47
A poem from Whitney	p48
A poem from Kelly	p50
Dominoes	p52
A poem from Shelley	p55
A haiku from Britney	p57
'Want to know how I got my name'	p58
A poem from Monsieur Nincompoop	p60
A candlestick	p61
Blank verse from the sous chef	p62
A sign	p65
'I wanted to write a poem about love'	p66
A medallion	p68
'As if I was going to ignore dis style of poetry'	p69
A Frogilo	p71
A poem from Olive	p72
Picture poetry	p77
A poem from a news reporter	p78
'When Mark da dog led us to dat allotment'	p80
A water bowl	p82

A poem that is actually a dance	p84
'Kids who say'	p86
A brick	p87
'Solar Pa'nelle is worried about pollution'	p88
Bookends	p90
'Yo. I was thinking about dis thing called poetry'	p92
A food bowl	p95
A poem from a very important special guest (even more important and special dan Solar Pa'nelle)	p96

Poetry hintroduction by Rapper Scool Yo

Yo. If you were one of da celebrities at da grand hopening of Chez Nincompoop, den you will know I is Rapper Scool Yo, and I is well famous. And my best mate, Pete, is not famous but he is tall and dat counts.

At da restaurant, I was hexplaining to Olive about why it is himportant for you and your friends to have your own hinterests, so dat you can do lots of things together but also things by yourself and with other people and whatnot.

Remember:　　　respect yourself

　　　　　　　　respect other people

　　　　　　　　and respect differences

And treat people how YOU would like to be treated. Dis is called karma and it is well cool. But back to da point of dis book. I is a rapper and I love poetry. Pete is not a rapper and he loves pottery. So while I is writing my hepic poems, he goes and spins bits of clay round and round on a little wheel.

We wanted to show you dat friends can (and should) do different things. I also was well pleased dat it was much easier to put da poetry in dis book dan it was da pottery, because of it being made out of clay and whatnot. Which proves dat poetry is better dan pottery, just saying.

To conclude dis bit, I is letting you know dat as well as some of my own hepic poems, lots of guest poets associated with Kids Club and Chez Nincompoop have contributed to dis book. I is well inclusive.

Yo. Respect.

Rapper Scool Yo

Pottery introduction by Pete

Hello there. My name is Pete. When my best friend, Rapper Scool Yo, told me he was writing a poetry book, I was slightly alarmed because even though he is my best friend, and a famous rapper, his English and grammar is frankly shocking, and I feared he would lead young minds astray with his dubious choice of words.

But after a heated discussion, I came to realise that grammar is not the ultimate priority, because poetry is a matter of expression. I'm not awfully keen on it myself, and much prefer pottery. The feeling of transforming a gloopy substance into a solid piece that can be a work of art, and a statement on society, but also a useful object is wondrous. If I'm feeling sad or worried or happy or impassioned, I rush to my potter's wheel and delve my hands into that glorious clay and pour my energy into creating something.

Which is why pottery is better than poetry. Especially if I've made a teapot, because then Rapper Scool Yo's nan may well invite me round for a cup of tea and a biscuit. However, as he has already pointed out, it proved quite tricky getting actual pots onto these pages, so we have gone with drawings of them instead. Very nice ones too. Look.

Pot on,
Pete

My grandma says my grammar is happalling

I say, nan, come on, I is hexpressing myself

She says, why can't you hexpress yourself by talking properly and using da correct pronunciation

I say, nan, language is evolving, and involving, and it's not a problem so stop your solving

She says, but your language sounds revolting

I say, nan, we all need a revolution now and den

She says, shall we have a cup of tea?

I say, only if we can have a biscuit an' all

She says, deal. And why not invite Pete. He's ever such a nice boy

A poem from Trixie

I'm Trixie

I'm pretty

My hair is really flicky

A book, oh yuck, of poetry

Don't care! Unless

The star is me?

Is it? Is it me?

Hello?

Rapper Scool Yo?

Honestleeeeeeeeeeee…

PETE'S POT ALERT!

I made a Toby Jug for Trixie (a Trixie Jug?) but unfortunately she wasn't that impressed and hurled it against a wall in a hissy fit. Still, a spot of glue works wonders

Pete is making some pots for me to grow herbs in

He says growing thyme is a good use of my time

I say, Pete, leave da rhymes to me

I can see myself being mates with basil, angelica and rosemary

And lavender is good for my aromatherapy

I'm down for jiving with chives

And chilling with dill

And without a doubt, it would be wise to grow sage

Fresh herbs are handy for when I'm cooking

Dusty packets won't get a look in

If it's right dere in a pot, won't have to forage for my borage

Question is – will it taste nice with porridge?

Mint, yeah, I can take a hint

Oregano? It's a yes, not a no

Coriander, for sure, it's a go

Marjoram is in da majority

But parsley? Personally I don't think so

PETE'S POT ALERT!
A bee hotel. Miss Squelch helped me with a bit of it. Well, some of it. Well, most of it. Thanks, Miss Squelch

A poem from Miss Squelch

Out in the garden, we dig! Dig! Dig!

Doesn't matter if the space is small or really big

Getting down in the mud makes us happy like a pig

It's even better than dancing at a Solar Pa'nelle gig

We create rows for our produce that don't zag and don't zig

And tend the worms in our wormery; watch them all wrig
              gle

Keep hydrated while you're working with lots of water – take a swig

If it's roasting, put on sunscreen; cover head with hat or wig

Lots of jobs in the garden: water, weed, snip off a sprig

Spread the compost, harvest veg, or just simply clear a twig

Won't hold you prisoner if you don't enjoy it, we won't take you to the brig

But we think you'll have a great time, full of energy and vig
               our

So join the Green Fingers Gang and help us grow tomatoes, cucumbers, aubergines, chillies, potatoes, radishes, beans, pumpkins, plums, apples, pears, and fig
               s

Get outdoors, grab a spade, and dig! Dig! Dig!

PETE'S POT ALERT!

Plant label sticks. Can you name all the veg that the Green Fingers Gang planted here?

When I was at school, I did not like science

It was really boring

What I did not know

Was dat science is heverything

Da way my hat stays on my head and does not fly off into space

Da gold dat my chain is made of

Da rapturous applause I receive when I has rapped

All of dis stuff is science

Chemistry and whatnot

Physics

Biology

And it is really really NOT boring

How did I not know dis at school? Dat chemical reactions and forces and gravity is all really cool?

Go straight to your science teacher and demand da most hexciting lesson ever – life

Just apply it

It's well scientific

Now, maths, dat's a whole different ball game

As is netball

PETE'S POT ALERT!
A thimble for Coach Outback's sewing kit (he's making a quilt. Using running stitch)

A limerick from Coach Outback*

There was a great coach who loved sport

Who upcycled much more than he bought

From whistles to medals

Cool quilts to bike pedals

And Frisbees that should always be caught

* Runner-up in the 1985 Blockedunnie Creek Poetry Slam

A sonnet from the headteacher

As Head, it's crucial to lead and inspire,
So I thought: I'll write a soulful sonnet,
But, oh! All it did was make me perspire,
Got worse and worse the longer spent on it.
In teaching, knowledge must be imparted,
Set pupils on paths that light up their way,
Facing a blank page? Just go; get started,
Express yourself! Find your voice! Have your say!
Because poetry – like music, like sport,
Like cooking, like art, like all those great things –
(Pie charts are important and should be taught),
But poems touch your soul and give you wings.
Sonnets though! Aaaaargh! All of those pesky rules!
Street dancing's more fun! Should be in all schools!

PETE'S POT ALERT!

A mosaic frame for the headteacher's school inspection certificate

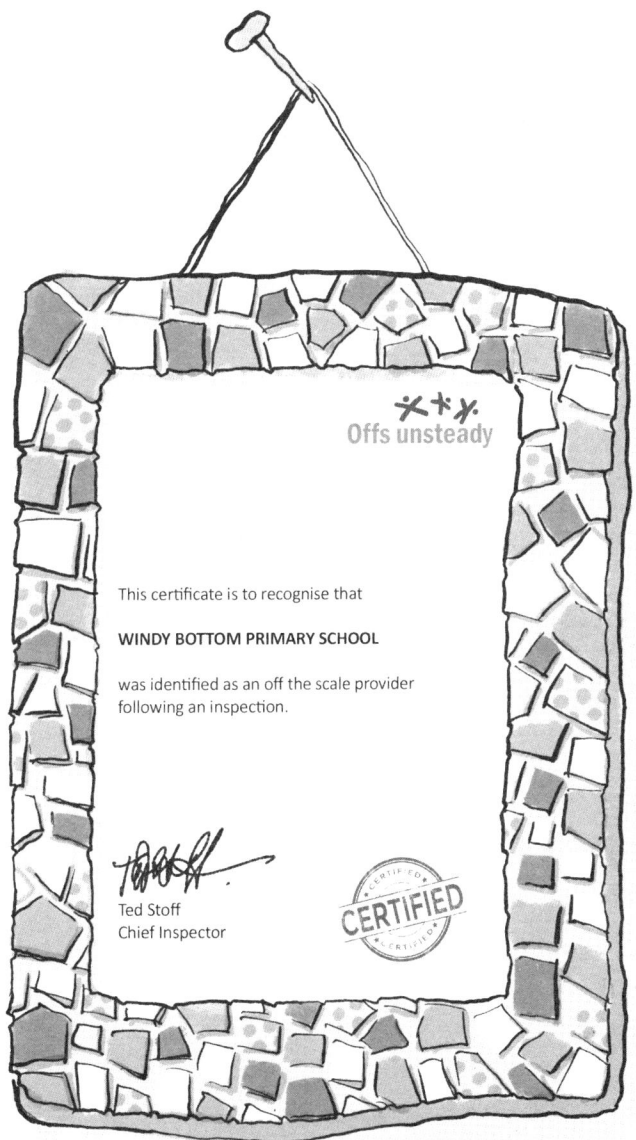

A poem from the dinner lady

Nothing is worse

Than writing in verse

To it, I'm averse

With my lips in a purse

Makes me cross and outraged and totally terse

It's just perverse

In fact, a curse

I feel like I'm going in reverse

In a hearse

Around the universe

And don't expect me to reimburse you for this offering

PETE'S POT ALERT!
A fridge magnet

Clamber

Shifty

Bellow, glorious, slab

Voluptuous

Portal, grasshopper

Crooked

Iguana, indigo

Ablaze, dangle, sunset, soar

Appliqué

Crumple, utmost

Flamboyant, fierce

Radiate

Prowl

Higgledy-piggledy

Hippopotamus

Wonky

I like dese words. Dey are well good. I think a list of words counts as a poem. Don't you?

A poem from Messy Jesse's mam entitled An Ode to Leftovers

For a whole lot of reasons, food waste is not funny

So with leftovers, well, here's the deal

In our house, we haven't got that much money

So I use up what's left in tomorrow night's meal

Jesse might mumble and sound off and grumble

But I can work wonders with canned beans and some herbs

And he's grateful enough when his tummy goes rumble

While he's studying science and irregular verbs

When times get too tough we rely on food banks

Too hungry to feel any shame

Yeah, we accept your donations with heartfelt thanks

And there are thousands all doing the same

But a change needs to come, we've got to wake up

And educate ourselves about food

Where it comes from, how much we need to take up

Because the awakening's rude

So make double portions, divide up and freeze

We all need to learn how to cook on a budget

Then another night's dinner will be a right breeze

Rescue a recipe if you've managed to fudge it

This isn't a lecture, it's not a mad rant

But a takeaway each day isn't the answer

Food: we must mind how we grow, store, transport, cook, eat, and plant

Especially if you're raising a growing dancer!

So rustle up summat nice for your tea

Must teach Jesse to cook – then HE can feed me!

A poem from Messy Jesse

Girls can be chefs, and boys can dance

We've got to believe and take a big chance

Just try, don't be shy; I'm sure that you'll fly

Especially if you wear some really big pants

PETE'S POT ALERT!
Wind chimes. Just because

Yo. I is a rapper, and I is a boy

But if I were a girl I could equally rap

Hobbies and jobs (and dolls and toys)

Go either way; don't fall into dat trap

of thinking dat blue is macho and hardy and male

and pink is all blushing and sweetness and pale

What rot!

We've got

to change da plot

and not

conform to ideologies and pressures placed on us in an outdated historical context by gender-biased patriarchal views dat reinforce da infrastructure of our society

Hmm. Dat line got away from me

Yo, we're all equal – anyone can fix cars

And be astronauts, wow, and visit da stars

(but not Mars, come on, dat's just going too far)

Girls and boys rock

Dey can be pilots of planes and pirates in boats

Designers of frocks, pants and fancy coats

Hairdressers, bakers, planters of trees

Teachers and poets and doctors of knees

(I am sure dat is a thing; if not, it should be)

We need scientists, yo, mad or not

And inventors, to invent lots of whatnot

Explorers of far distant lands, or da 'hood

Boys and girls can both do it, dey're equally good

Superheroes – should dey be he or she?

As long as a sparkly cape's involved, EITHER, frankly

So if you're a girl who dreams of becoming a chef

Or a boy who loves dancing to a treble clef

Rise up! Take dat step! My friends, fly free!

Equality. Equality. And quality tea

A poem from Messy Jesse's dance teacher

In my dance class, there are nine girls
They flit, do splits, and endless twirls
They love to move, they shout and shriek
And breathlessly return each week
But front and centre, look closely
At the dancer there, can you see?
Tipping scales of equality
(I grant you, only just slightly)
Who is it, pray, who can it be?
None other than Messy Jesse!
As much as girls, he loves to dance
And proves it, given half a chance
Enthusiasm unmatched here
He has no nerves, he knows no fear
Just watch him dance, just watch him go
Each move filled with utter gusto
He skids! Slides! Off walls he bounces
Daring steps with sudden flounces

The music booms; he's never bored
Choreography? No! Ignored!
The girls all laughed, at first unkind
He carried on, he didn't mind
His joy of dance is great and vast
Look how he spins on his way past!
Limbs flail wide, so deep in rapture
Flying high, he's hard to capture
Technique is off, his style is wrong
Jesse dances to his own song
But for pride and effort? Well, then –
Top marks! Yes, it's ten out of ten!

PETE'S POT ALERT!
Coat pegs for Messy Jesse's dance class

Have a go at blackout poetry, yo! Choose a harticle from a newspaper or photocopy a page from a book, read through for words or phrases you fancy, den scribble out da rest to leave a hepic poem. Don't try it in an actual book though – especially not DIS book

> ~~~~~~~~ Grandma, dangling ~~~~~
> ~~~~~~~~ fingertips ~~~~~~~~~~~~~
> ~~~~~~~~~~~~~~~~~~~~~~~~~~~~~~~~~
> ~~~~~~~~~~~
> ~~~~~~ slowly turned ~~~~~~~~~~~~
> ~~~~~~~~~~~~~~~~~~~~~~~~~~~~~~~~~
> ~~~~~~ began to crackle with electricity ~~~~~~~
> grey and natural and tangled with treasure; ~~~~~~
> ~~~~~~~~~~~~ proud.
>
> ~~~~~~ is that you? ~~~~~~~~~~~
> ~~~~~~~~~~~~~~~~~~~~~~~~~~~~~~
> ~~~~ the best ~~~~~~~~~~~~~~~~~~~~
> best friend."
>
> ~~~~~~~~~~~~~~~~~~~~~~~~~~~~~~~~~
> ~~~~~~ You haven't changed. ~~~~~~~~~
> ~~~~~~~~~~~~~~~~~~~~~~~~~~
> ~~~~~~~~~~~~~~~~~~~ Grandma ~~~~,
> ~~~~~~~~~~ held it close to her heart.
> "I am here ~~~~~~~~~~~~~~~~~~~~~~
> ~~~~~~~~~~~~~~~
> She was here. ~~~~~~~~~~~~~~~~~
> ~~~~~~~~~~~~~~~~~~~~~~~~~~~~~~~~
> ~~~~~~~~~~~~~~~~~~~~~~~~~~~~ too.

A poem from Whitney

There's a flaw in the floor

Can you draw a drawer?

If a boulder got bolder, would wood too?

Don't steal steel

Never meet meat

Is a cotton reel real?

Don't bare your teeth at a bare bear

Or bore a wild boar on a surfboard

Never foul foul fowl who are playing football or stalk a stork on a beanstalk

You mustn't groan at a grown-up

Or compare a pair of pears with a paring knife

Is the fare at the fayre fair?

And the same for a fete? Who knows? Fate? Life?

When is a grate great?

Can you wait for a weight?

I heard a herd, saw a sore saw, had a peek at a peak

I've also gazed in awe at an oar... or have I?

Please pause while I pour pawpaw sauce over a poor paw and pore over the pores in my perfect skin

So, can you sow seeds? Or sew on sequins?

I hear you over here

As for over there, they're letting their ears flare with flair

I'm sure about the shore

Where would you wear your ware?

Would you roll a roll around a role?

Have you ever fought in a fort? Or sought out a different sort?

Might a doe eat dough? And roar if it were raw?

I've whirled my way around this world

And now, our hour is up

One more thing, though – I like to read beside reeds

But are you reading this in Reading?

Because that is a different story

A poem from Kelly

Some days I feel like I just don't fit in

Some days I feel all wrong in my skin

Nippity-noppity

I squirm on the inside

I struggle to breathe

I loosen my collar

I sigh and I heave

Nippity-noppity

Some days I feel the whole world is against me

Some days I feel I am totally wonky

I blister with turmoil

I burble with rage

I'm trapped here inside me

My very own cage

It's hard to pinpoint

It's hard to explain

It's not outwardly obvious, this kind of pain

These days are not good days

These days are not fun

I don't want to take part, talk to anyone

Nippity-noppity

But there are other days

Better days

Good days

Great days

Nippity-noppity

Some days you just have to let go

PETE'S POT ALERT!

I made a set of dominoes for Kids Club. Shelley and Kelly have been playing an epic game! Who will win?

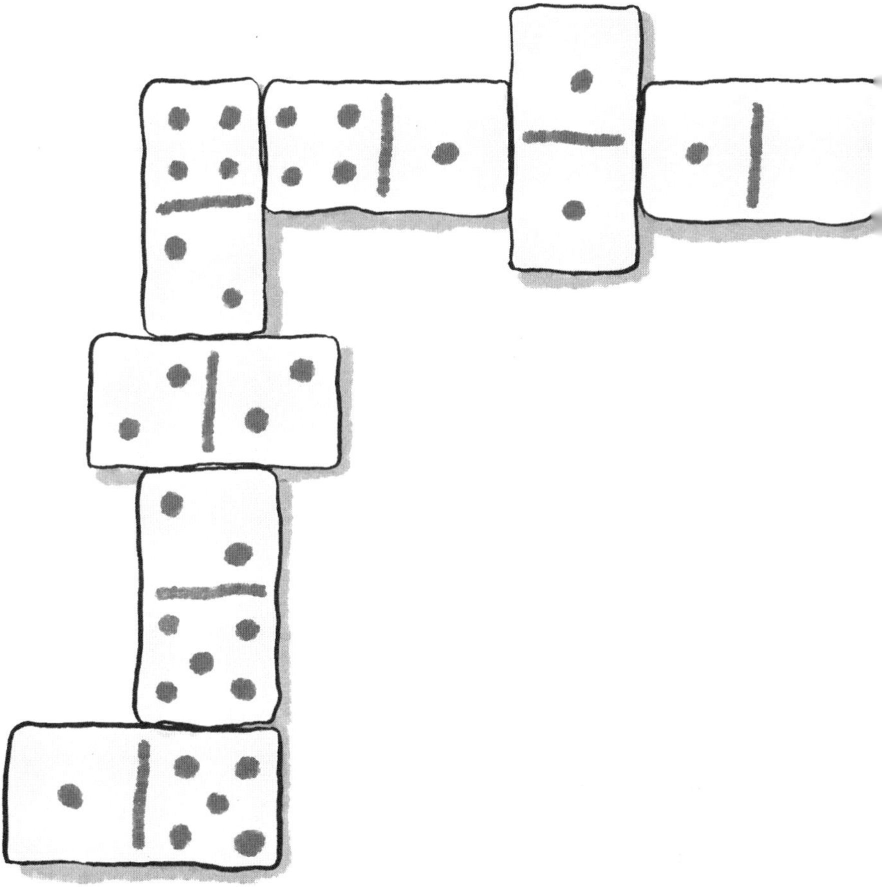

A poem from Shelley

Some people think

That girls should have long hair

And wear pink

And be clean

And sweet

And helpful and neat

And should smile and be peacekeepers

And not upset the equilibrium

I think

That these things are fine

But I also want to scuff my shoes and spill things and discover new horizons and fill my pockets with treasure such as paperclips and conkers and pictures of zebras

And climb trees in my stripy trousers and eat cherries

And have short hair

A haiku from Britney

You might have guessed that

I'd be the one to master

A harder art form

Want to know how I got my name – Rapper Scool Yo?

I is a rapper. I is cool. And I is always learning Yo. So dere you go. Now you know

Just to be clear –

It is not da same as Rapper Scowl Yo

He is a rival of mine and he always scowls at me

Or Rapper Shawl Yo

He wears a shawl dat he knit himself

Or Rapper Skill Yo

Man, he has got no skills. Just ignore him

Or Rapper Skull Yo and her brother, Rapper Scalp Yo

Dey have to be careful with their hats

Or Rapper Scale Yo

Musical scales not fish scales. We leave dem to Rapper School of Fish Yo. He is well fishy

Or Rapper Scald Yo

I keep telling him to watch out around kettles

Or Rapper Scarf Yo

(She is jealous of Rapper Shawl Yo)

Or Rapper Scout Yo

Dib dib dib

Or Rapper Stool Yo

Don't sit on him. He gets cross. Like his mate, Rapper Scold Yo

Or Rapper Scone Yo

Now, him we like. But he disagrees with Rapper Scot Yo on how to pronounce his name

Or Rapper Spool Yo

She finds it hard to unwind

Or Rapper Spoil Yo

No spoilers, please

Or Rapper Spoon Yo

He's well handy

Or Rapper Snail Yo

It took him a while to get here

A poem from Monsieur Nincompoop

Bonsoir!

Je m'appelle Monsieur Nincompoop

'ere is my recipe

In ze form of poetry

Take one celebrity chef – make sure 'e is very 'andsome and very stylish

Grow lots of delicious organic vegetables

Cook zem with 'erbs and season zem well

Serve with a flourish

Et voila!

BUT!

Just make sure ze sous chef employed

Washes 'is 'ands! Or it will all be destroyed!

PETE'S POT ALERT!

Fancy restaurants often have candles on their tables. I made this candlestick for Chez Nincompoop, taking inspiration from the chef's hat. Can you spot it?

Blank verse from the sous chef at Chez Nincompoop

Deep, wasn't it?

PETE'S POT ALERT!
A sign for the toilets at Chez Nincompoop

I wanted to write a poem about love

Not da kind you have for your nan or your bruv

But da kind that encases you like a snugly warm glove

Embrace it, give lots of it, especially when push comes to shove

We all need it. We all have it to give. Love

I wanted to write a poem about time

Not da kind dat you get in a pot (dat's called thyme)

But da kind you can't capture in just one little rhyme

Da point is - don't waste it, dat's truly a crime

Be aware of it. Spend it wisely. Time

I wanted to write a poem about sharing

Not da kind you don't do when you're tight and not caring

Generosity rocks, it's brilliant and daring

If you don't share, you'll see me in da corner, glaring

Share. Share everything! Go on. Get sharing

While I write those poems, I would love to share dis one with you if you have da time?

PS Love makes da world go round

Just like da clay on Pete's little wheel

Should you ever get restless or bored

Remember: da pen is mightier dan da sword

PETE'S POT ALERT!
When I first started pottery classes, I wanted to make a present for my best friend, Rapper Scool Yo. I asked him what he'd like. He suggested a china medallion for his gold chain. There was a slight misunderstanding, but he still wears it proudly

As if I was going to ignore dis style of
$$\text{poetry}$$

Cultured to da core, yo, dat is me

Rapaciously rapping and setting words free

Occasionally stopping for a nice cup of tea

Sometimes I wonder if I should switch to
$$\text{pottery}$$

Throw some clay, make a plate, style it up, out-pot Pete

It might be nice to delve in and get my hands dirty

Crazy talk! Not gonna happen

People often say to me

Oh! Rapper Scool Yo!

Ever thought about releasing a book of poetry?

Truthfully! Dey could not have known dat with every breath I am

Releasing poetry. Unleashing poetry. Thing is though – are

YOU gonna unleash some?

PETE'S POT ALERT!

A Frogilo for Olive's grandad's allotment. Attracting wildlife to gardens is crucial, but they also need a safe place from predators. Can you spot any wildlife in your nearest outdoor space?

A poem from Olive

There is something I want to tell my best friend

And it's really hard

Face to face

So I thought I'd write it down

Here goes

Trixie

For as long as I can remember, you have been the one that I wanted to be friends with

It felt like a badge of honour

The best badge that could be worn

And I let it go on for far too long

The constant putting me down

The ways in which you would tell me I'm not good enough

What a loser I am

How rubbish I am

How wonky I am

No

I am good enough

It took me a long time to learn this

And I wish

I wish

I wish I'd been braver sooner

I'm worn out

For all the times you made me do something I didn't want to do, cajoling me, bribing me

Threatening me

No

For all the times you made me feel small, and worthless

And wrong

No

For all the times you hurt me

No

No

NO

But

→

←

For all the times you made me laugh

Properly laugh, side-splitting, got-a-stitch laugh

The times you made me feel needed

The times you made me feel cool

The times you made me feel chosen

Thank you

You told me people are weird and stupid

You meant people who weren't YOU

People are complicated, aren't they?

YOU are complicated

But this is okay

Because now I am brave

Maybe one day you'll invite me round to your house after school and not mind that I've been to gardening club first

Or that I've got dirt under my fingernails

Maybe one day you'll support my cooking

Even if you don't like the taste

Maybe one day we'll dance together

A routine that we both make up

Maybe

You're Trixie

You're pretty

Your hair is… quite flicky

I want you to be my friend

But I'm telling you I am my own best friend now

And the badge that I wear is a wonky one

PS No-one knows this but you were the one who taught me how to ride a bike

Thank you

Sometimes you might not feel in da mood for writing a hepic poem. Get inspired by nature instead, innit. Find a well nice picture, photocopy it, and you'll be scribbling in no time

A symbol of
summer
Standing tall and
proud
Nodding
Smiling
Reflecting
da sun

A poem from Rosalind, an intrepid news reporter

Newsflash! Hooray! A feel-good story!

(A rarity when so much is horrid and gory)

The tale of Olive, triumphant and brave

In which a trail was blazed, a way was paved

She saved the day at Chez Nincompoop

For this jaded journalist, it's a peach of a scoop

A child who stepped up when the chips were down

And cooked up a storm! She's the toast of the town!

Reporting the news can often be bad

Out there each day with my pen and my pad

Searching for truth when the pickings are slim

Sometimes this world can be harsh and so grim

Which is why we must strive for the positive bits

The joy and the wonder, the greatest hits

Working hard and being kind pays off it seems

Trying your best, believing in dreams

Be decent and honest; steer clear of trouble

Look for the glory amongst all the rubble

Revel in times that give cheer and delight

You've got this.
        Like Olive, turn your face to the light

When Mark da dog led us to dat allotment

I could not believe my eyes

Da surprise

When I realised

Dat vegetables grew in da ground

And did not just magically happear in da freezer or in tins like da ones in my nan's cupboard above her sink

It took a while to sink in

We has got to look after da ground

So dat da vegetables can keep growing

And da rivers can keep flowing

And da wind can keep blowing

Da ground is basically earth

Planet Earth

It's our only home and it is worth

More than stuff and stretch limos and gold chains and whatnot

We has got to look after it

Now open up YOUR eyes

Da earth is da top prize

We has got to save it, brave it out

Come on, help me shout

Respect da earth

Think about da stuff you buy

And da stuff you chuck away

FOR

    DERE

        IS

           NO

              AWAY

I repeat - respect da earth

Without it, we would be well stuffed

And would not be able to grow vegetables

Including stuffed peppers

Dis does not mean you should not buy my new halbum

Just saying

PETE'S POT ALERT!
A water bowl for Mark the dog. Woof

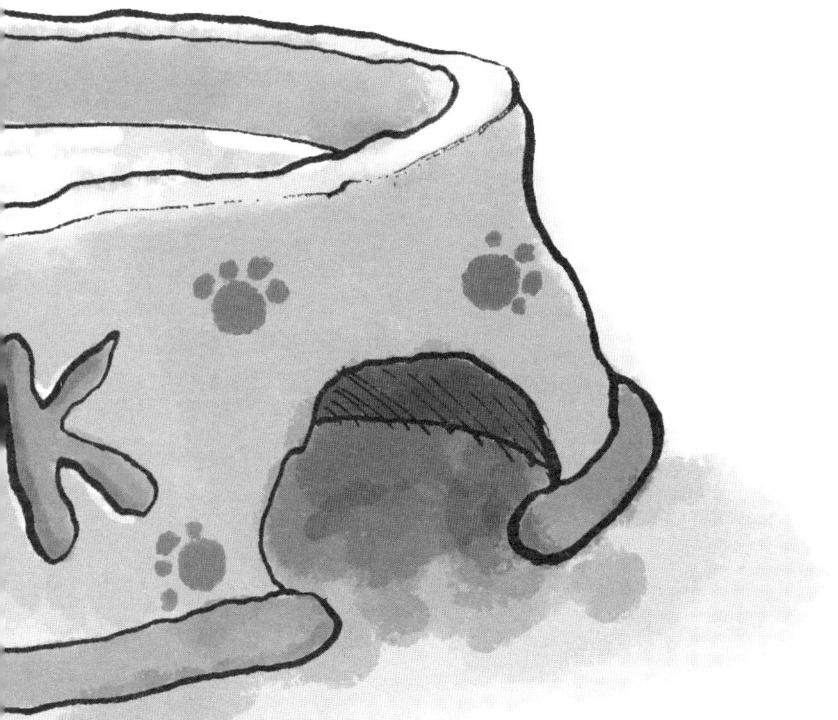
K

A poem that is actually a dance (look out for the routine featuring on Solar Pa'nelle's new pop video)

5

6

5 6 7 8

Plant the seed

Plant the seed

Plant the seed

Plant the seed

Down comes the rain

Down comes the rain

Down comes the rain

Down comes the rain

The sun shines

The sun shines

The sun shines

The sun shines

Plant starts to grow

Plant starts to grow

Plant starts to grow

Plant starts to grow

Whoop for the plant

Whoop whoop

Whoop for the plant

Whoop whoop

Whoop for the plant

Whoop whoop

Whoop for the plant

Kids who say

Dey don't like poetry

Should know

Dat poetry likes dem

PETE'S POT ALERT!
A brick. Just because. (Solar Pa'nelle uses it as a doorstop in her dressing room. She's very welcoming)

Solar Pa'nelle is worried about pollution

She says, Rapper Scool Yo, what could be da solution

I say, Solar, my friend, I do not know

Yo yo yo yo yo yo yo yo yo. Yo

She is aghast about all da plastic

She says, Rapper Scool Yo, da problem is drastic

I say, Solar, we have all just got to say no

Yo yo yo yo yo yo yo yo yo. Yo

She is concerned about da forest of rain

She says, Rapper Scool Yo, cutting it down causes pain

I say, Solar, each fell is a major blow

Yo yo yo yo yo yo yo yo yo. Yo

She's a child of dis planet and wants no more burning

She says, Rapper Scool Yo, we must keep da earth turning

I say, Solar, we all want to bask in your glow

Yo yo yo yo yo yo yo yo yo. Yo

She is alarmed about factory farming

She says, Rapper Scool Yo, animals are not ours to be harming

I say, Solar, okay, have a vegan dough
                              nut

Yo yo yo yo yo yo yo yo yo. But
   remember to not get overwhelmed by all da problems and forget to enjoy yourself. Yo

Solar Pa'nelle says, Rapper Scool Yo, you are right (I say, I know, I am always right), we must count our blessings

She says, live life! Without leaving nasty messings

I say, Solar, I'm happy to go with your flow

Yo yo yo yo yo yo yo yo yo. Yo

PETE'S POT ALERT!
Bookends for Rapper Scool Yo's eclectic collection

POETRY BY
POETRY by ROOMY
A book of Poetry by
ROGER COUGHED
Collected Poems
Verse by Michael Raisin
DOROTHY PARKBENCH
COLLECTED POEMS

Yo. I was thinking about dis thing called poetry

And how it is for you and definitely for me

I kind of like a rhyme

But sometimes not

And dat is okay

What?

Is you da rhyme police?

But when all's said and done

And it is time for bed

Sometimes I want to let out da stuff in my head

It's all whirling and swirling

Around in dere

Underneath my hat, underneath my hair

So I write it all down

It gives me some space

I don't need it to be right

Or proper

Or ace

(Although it always is, because I is a well cool rapper)

So my hadvice to you

Is to give it a go

I believe in you, yeah

I is Rapper Scool Yo

PETE'S POT ALERT!

There are so many other things I've made that we didn't have the space to include here, such as a dish for Olive to 'dish da dish' in, a stand for Messy Jesse's headphones, a sign for Kids Club, a garden gnome, some jugs, several vases, a holder for licked spoons in the kitchen at Chez Nincompoop, a cameo brooch featuring Solar Pa'nelle in profile, a display stand for this book, countless mugs (including one with a reminder to check my shoelaces), tiles, a pizza oven, and a clay pigeon. (I also attempted to make some pottery pants for the scarecrow. Really big ones. How do you think that went?)

What would YOU like to make? And there are so many other artistic ways to get involved – decorating your pottery, drawing pictures of it, dancing round the room with it...

Get crafty – I'd love to see your artwork, and prove that pottery is better than poetry! Send it to me on Twitter **@reallybptheatre** or Facebook using **Really Big Pants Theatre** or via the Really Big Pants website **reallybigpants.co.uk**

In the meantime, here's a food bowl I made for Roger (the school's pet rat)

A poem from a very important special guest – YOU

Yo. You and I both know you're going to write an awesome poem on dese pages. Share it with me via dat lot at Really Big Pants and let's show Pete dat poetry is better dan pottery. Go for it. Yo